First Position
Scale Studies
for
the Violin
book one - expanded edition

by Cassia Harvey

Contents

G Major: First Octave...................... 2
D Major: First Octave...................... 6
A Major: Second Octave.................. 10
C Major: First Octave...................... 14
G Major: Second Octave.................. 18
B-Flat Major: First Octave................ 22
F Major: First Octave...................... 26
A Major: First Octave...................... 30
E Major: First Octave...................... 34
B Major: Second Octave.................. 38
B-Flat Major: Second Octave.............. 42
E-Flat Major: First Octave................ 46
A-Flat Major: First Octave................ 50
Scales to Play With Vibrato................ 54
Fast Scale Studies......................... 59
Major Scales in First Position............. 66
Building Major Arpeggios.................. 69
Major Arpeggios in First Position.......... 74

CHP317

©2021 by C. Harvey Publications All Rights Reserved.

www.charveypublications.com - print books
www.learnstrings.com - PDF downloadable books
www.harveystringarrangements.com - chamber music

G Major: First Octave

Cassia Harvey

Slurs

Scale Rhythms

Dotted Quarter Note Rhythms

D Major: First Octave

Slurs

Scale Rhythms

6/8 Timing

A Major: Second Octave

Slurs

Scale Rhythms

Trills

C Major: First Octave

Slurs

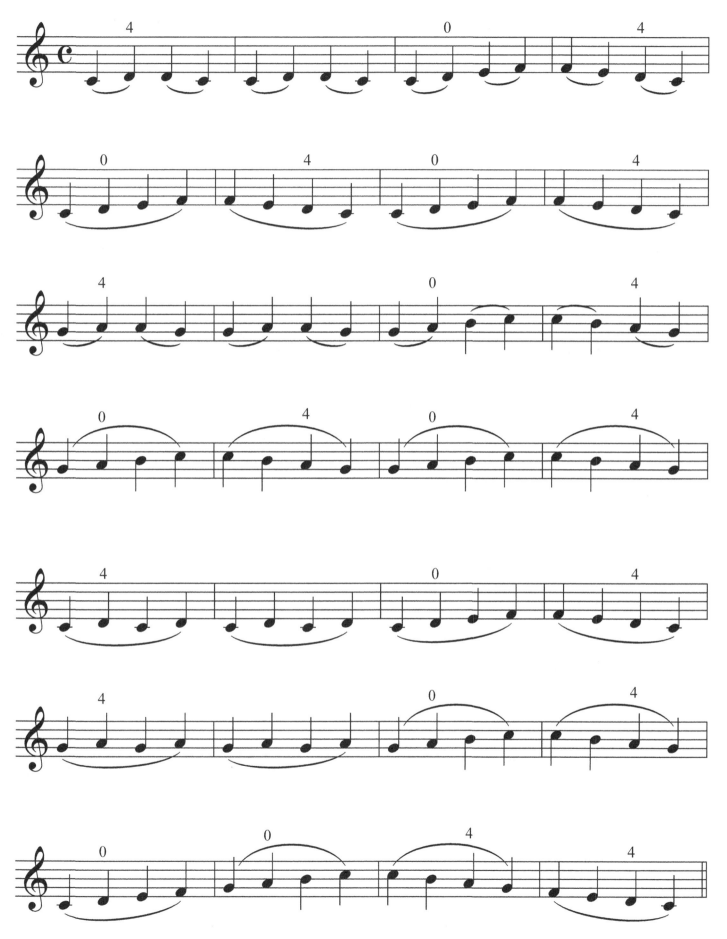

Dotted Quarter Note Rhythms

6/8 Timing

G Major: Second Octave

Slurs

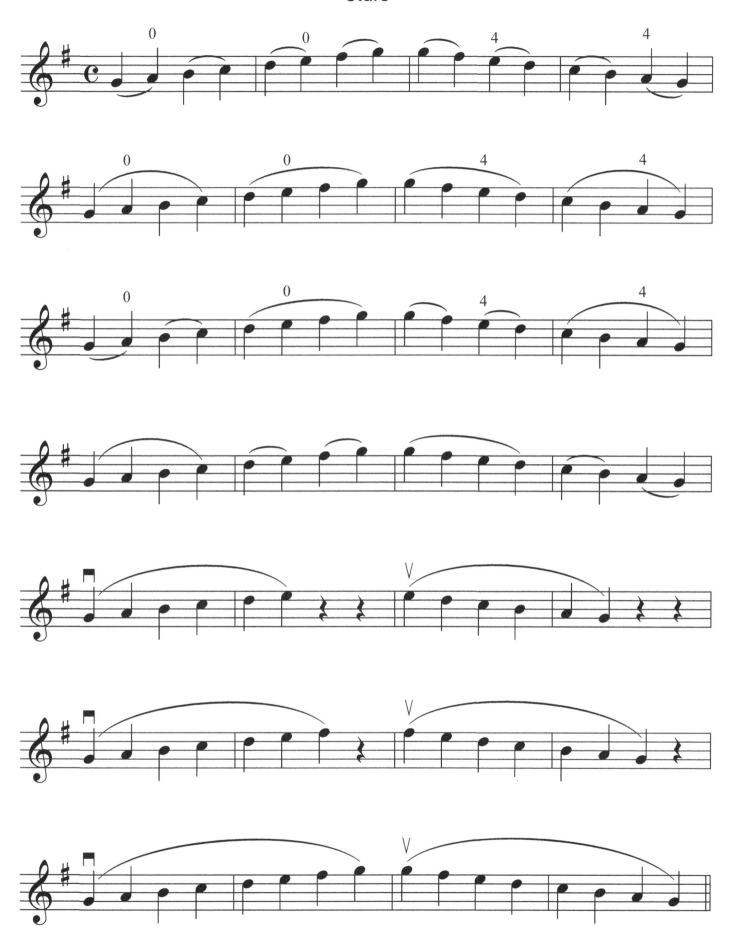

Dotted Quarter Note Rhythms

6/8 Timing

B♭ Major: First Octave

Scale Rhythms

Slurs

Scale Finger Workout

F Major: First Octave

Slurs

Dotted Quarter Note Rhythms

3/4 Timing

A Major: First Octave

Slurs

Scale Rhythms

Slurs in 3/4 Timing

E Major: First Octave

Slurs

Scale Rhythms

6/8 Timing

B Major: Second Octave

Slurs

Scale Rhythms

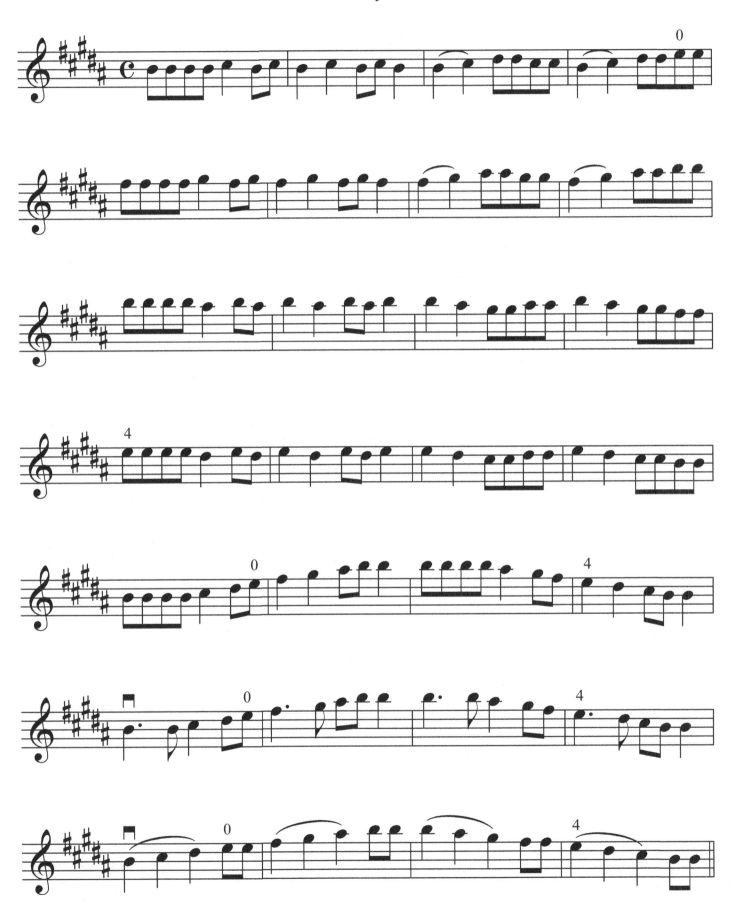

6/8 Timing

B♭ Major: Second Octave

Slurs

Scale Rhythms

6/8 Timing

E♭ Major: First Octave

Slurs

Scale Rhythms

Pickups

A♭ Major: First Octave

Slurs and Ties

Scale Rhythm and Slur Combinations

5/4 Timing

Scales to play with Vibrato

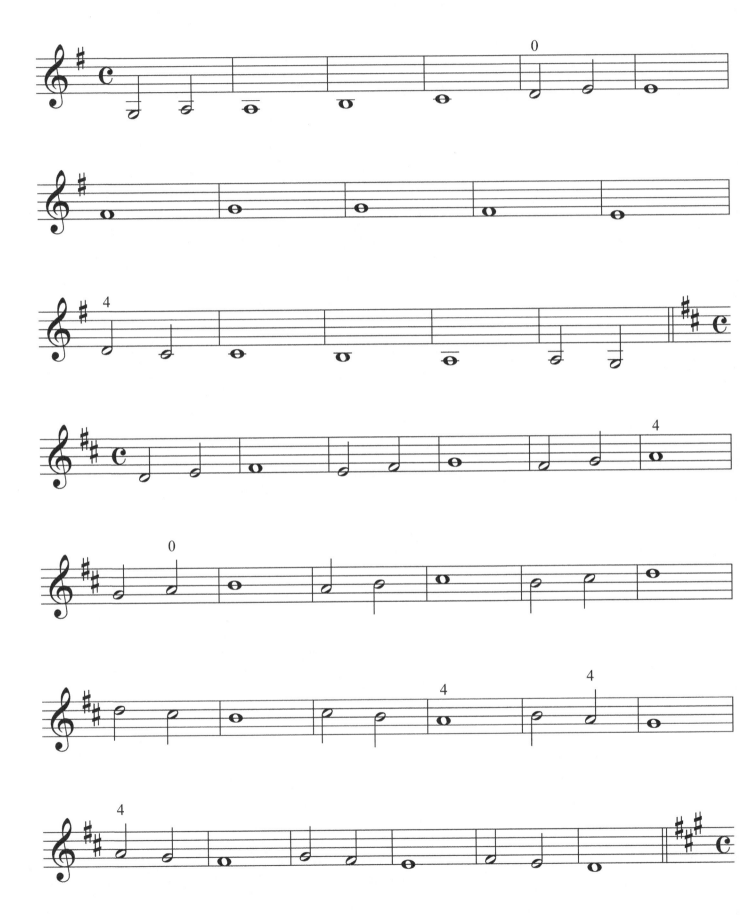

Fast Scale Studies

Major Scales in First Position

G Major

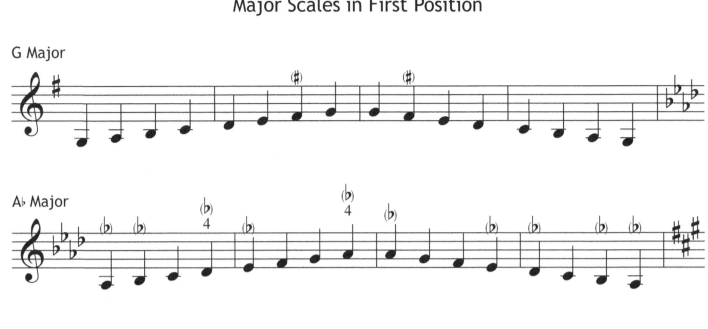

A♭ Major

A Major

B♭ Major

B Major

C Major

Db Major

D Major

Eb Major

E Major

F Major

F# Major

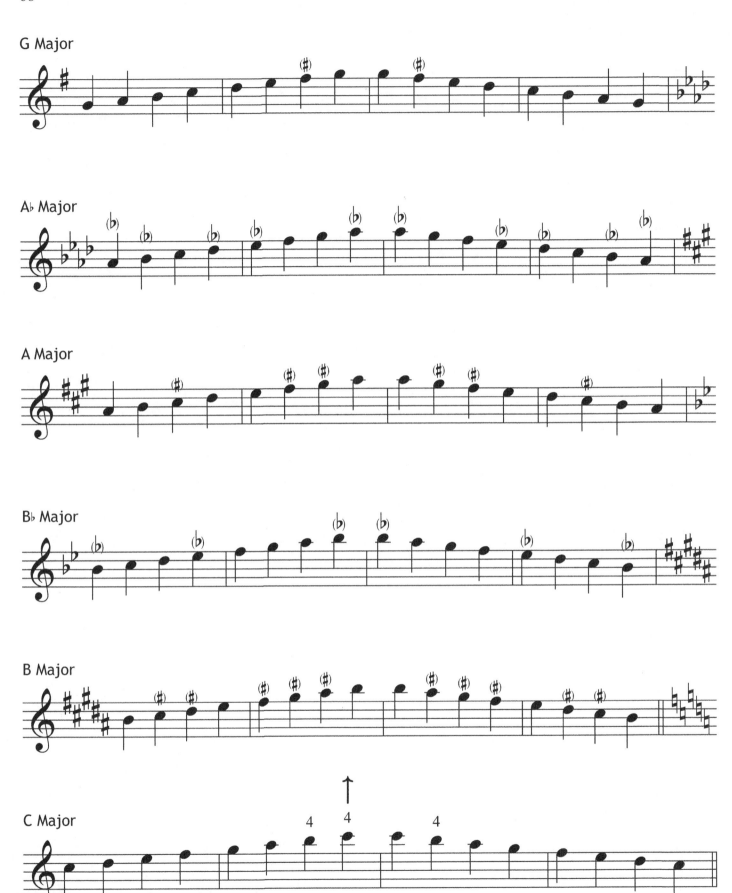

G Major

A♭ Major

A Major

B♭ Major

B Major

C Major

From Scale to Arpeggio: The Large Notes form a Major Arpeggio

Building Major Arpeggios in First Position

B♭ Major

B Major

C Major

D♭ Major

D Major

E♭ Major

E Major

F Major

F# Major

G Major

A♭ Major

A Major

B♭ Major

B Major

C Major

Major Arpeggios in First Position

2

Beginning Fiddle Duets for Two Violins

Cripple Creek

Trad., arr. Myanna Harvey

Available from www.charveypublications.com
The Blackberry Blossom Fiddle Book for Violin

Table of Contents

How to Use This Book..3

1. Harvest Home: First Warm-Up..........................4
2. Harvest Home: Second Warm-Up......................5
3. Harvest Home..6
4. Blackberry Blossom: First Warm-Up...................8
5. Blackberry Blossom: Second Warm-Up................9
6. Blackberry Blossom...10
7. The Dashing Sergeant: First Warm-Up...............12
8. The Dashing Sergeant: Second Warm-Up...........13
9. The Dashing Sergeant.....................................14
10. Old Joe Clark: First Warm-Up.........................16
11. Old Joe Clark: Second Warm-Up.....................17
12. Old Joe Clark..18
13. King of the Fairies: First Warm-Up..................20
14. King of the Fairies: Second Warm-Up...............21
15. King of the Fairies...22
16. The Blarney Pilgrim: First Warm-Up.................24
17. The Blarney Pilgrim: Second Warm-Up.............25
18. The Blarney Pilgrim.......................................26
19. The Parting Blessing: Warm-Up.......................28
20. The Parting Blessing......................................29
21. Leather Breeches: First Warm-Up....................30
22. Leather Breeches: Second Warm-Up................31
23. Leather Breeches..32
24. The Rakes of Kildare: First Warm-Up...............34
25. The Rakes of Kildare: Second Warm-Up...........35
26. The Rakes of Kildare.....................................36
27. Big John McNeil: First Warm-Up.....................38
28. Big John McNeil: Second Warm-Up.................38
29. Big John McNeil..40
30. The Red-Haired Boy: First Warm-Up................42
31. The Red-Haired Boy: Second Warm-Up............43
32. The Red-Haired Boy......................................44

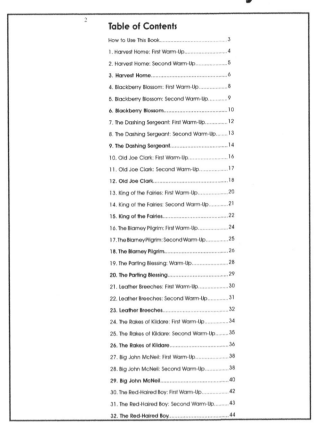

Fiddle Exercises at two different levels.

Fiddle Tunes at two different levels can be played solo, in duets, or in chamber ensembles.

Exercises, Tunes, and Harmonies are compatible with the viola, cello, and string bass books!

Made in the USA
Monee, IL
31 December 2022

24104375R00044